Shimmering Brilliance

Desiree Batiste

Self-published by Desiree Batiste

This book is dedicated to so many wonderful people in my life!

First and foremost, this is dedicated to God - as without his love and the gift of my talent, I would not be where I am today. I know I owe him everything and I hope that in some small measure I am helping to 'pay it forward' to others and give them the love and understanding that they deserve.

My husband, Michael...I couldn't have done this without your love and support. You are my love and one of my sources of inspiration and I love you so much!

My daughter Kaylee and son Aaron...you guys have been my cheering section throughout this journey, and I thank you for keeping me motivated.

To my four cats: Sketch, Pixel, Trace and Slim Shady...you guys are four legged little angels full of mischief and love and your presence everyday has been like a soothing blanket.

To all of my fans...who bought "The Shaping of a Diamond"... You were touched by the poems and felt that connection, which was exactly what I wanted to happen. I hope that my story inspires others to know that they are worth more than their circumstances and they have the power to want and have a better life.

To my followers on Instagram, TikTok, Twitter, Goodreads, Booksie, Medium and all of my supporters and fellow group members on Facebook... Thank you for making "the newbie" feel welcome in this new world of being a published author. So many of my poems ended up being published online and in print and I am beyond thankful for the community rallying around me and seeing value in my work.

To Amy and Charity of Immortal Trees bookstore in Avondale, AZ...thanks for making me one of your resident poets/authors and for so thoroughly promoting my last book. I can't wait to see what happens with this one.

Let's hope that this journey will also be a connection to the souls of all those who need someone that understands and this circle of love around me will grow just a little more.

Thank you Everyone!!!

Contents

Content Warning

This book explores aspects of mental health challenges and contains depictions of self-harm, physical and sexual abuse. These aspects may be difficult for some readers. **Please read with care.**

Images

All images used in this book are royalty-free, available for public download and use and were obtained legally for that purpose.

Realm 1: Shadows of the Past

It's true anyone who is healing from a traumatic past will still see the shadows of it looming in the distance somewhere. That is the perverse magic of PTSD – like a time machine, it carries you back to these awful moments in time and it feels just like the first time. If you have read my first book, "The Shaping of a Diamond", then you will understand exactly what I am talking about. These poems cover some of those very shadows which have crossed my path from time to time. I know forgetting is never going to be an option, so now I just channel my feelings to this creative venue and at least try to make something beautiful or profound come out of my horrid experiences and memories. These seven realms I am about to take you on a journey through are the ones in which I spend most of my time every day. At the end of this first realm, if you find yourself relating to my words, then high-five time! We truly are in this together and you are not alone!

Closed Doors*

I grew up with apprehension
once I wasn't someone she'd adore
I'd brace myself for the tension
each time she closed the door

Then the pastor's son
out looking to score
said the 'game' we'd play would be fun
as he quickly closed the door

Being abused by my son's father
until I could take no more
Worse always went farther
every time he closed the door

My first husband was evil
He almost killed me, as I lay on the floor
He moved out after his belonging's retrieval
while I was relieved that behind him, he closed the door

My third husband went to jail
his humanity, extremely poor
Every time he approached, I paled
praying he wasn't about to close the door

After he left, he played mind games

trying to rekindle what I had felt before

but I knew things could never be the same

and had the courage to close the door

When I met my soulmate, I knew

I'd never felt this way before

and that I could start life anew

All I had to do…was close the door

*This poem was first printed in August of 2023 in "Imspired" magazine. It was featured in Issue 24 and the Volume 12 Print Edition which was released at the end of September 2023. Big thanks to Steve Cawte for helping me share it with the world!

Darkest Before the Dawn

The sunset of my childhood
marked the birth of adulthood
but as I held his hand
the shadows began to form
More and more of them
until I knew this was the sunset
of my own happiness

I lived in the darkness
with the beatings
the insults
the fornication
No matter whose
hand I held
the darkness only grew

A sentence of
20 years to life
was my punishment
for trying to love
the wrong men
Those who are
so damned that
they are undeserving
of anyone's love

Then 2020 rolled around

and in the fall
hints of light
began to appear
His aura was so different
He was genuine with
his thoughts, feelings
and actions

As my love for him grew
the lock on my
self-made prison
sprung open
and the brightest
sunrise ever seen
filled my vision
My life since
has been filled
with mostly light
Shadows did try to
creep back in
like they always do
but it was just the sun
passing behind some
clouds, then bursting
back out, shining its
brilliance for all
to see

It is true

what they say

It is always darkest

before the dawn

Just never give up

and know that

your own

shimmering brilliance

is going to find you

and burn all

the darkness away

Evergreen

Such a basic tree

Ordinary but beautiful

A real-life reflection of myself

This tree of evergreen

Once upon a time, my only
source of comfort

It's been there my whole life

How many times I sought shade

Under the evergreen

When the days passed so fast

But the nights were so long

I'd miss the time I'd stolen away

Under the evergreen

Away from her piercing glare

Out of reach of her grasp

I knew that I was safe

Under the evergreen

Finally came the day

I got to leave that life behind
But I knew I'd never forget the solace found
Under the evergreen

So many years gone by
and I often catch myself asking
Is there now another broken girl sitting
Under the evergreen?

If its branches shielded me, they can protect you
It has a quiet wisdom
a way of helping you find answers
Under the evergreen

So daydream, in that park
Bask in the warmth of the sun
and treasure every moment spent
Under the evergreen

Invisible

Am I here?
Keep trying to grasp
onto something real
so I can tell that
I'm still alive
You just look
right through me
as if I were invisible

Perhaps I am
You don't seem
to see the real me
smell my fear
feel my sadness
or taste my tears

Now I'm left wondering
whether I've disappeared
completely or
just from your care
your sight

your heart

How am I supposed
to know what's real anymore
when your love
was the only constant
that I've believed in
all these years?

Please tell me
nothing has changed
and that you still
know my heart
belongs with yours!

Nothing can separate us
unless something becomes
more important than
our love and comes
between us

As long as I
draw breath
nothing will take
the place of you
as my other half

I'll always see
your beautiful eyes
and hope the next
time I check
they're looking at me,
not through me

It Should Have Been Her

Time passes
but with a vast difference
Sometimes you wish
a certain time could
last forever
and other times
wish for salvation
from the horrible moments

Yet, time is perverse
it speeds up happy moments
creating just a blur
and slows time
for that which we don't
wish to experience

My hate-filled mother
for example
Why couldn't she have
been the one that
passed away?

I carry sixteen years
of silent screams

Then, five years later
my father left this world
casting me into a sea
of morose nightmares
re-living how she killed him
with wet diamonds trailing
down my cheeks

He has now been gone
longer than he was here
with me
It should have been her
Twenty-three years was the cost
robbed of time that belonged to us
Twenty-three years of sorrow
nailed me down to the ground
Years she didn't deserve

Death, how could you
make such an egregious error?
This irreversible pain...
it should have been her
It should have been her

Never Home

It never felt like home
as an awkward child
so out of place

I used to dream about where I'd
go
My imagination running wild
As tears streamed down my face

Bullies who taunted me
A house full of secrets
Darkness loomed in every corner

I can hear her hateful voice – it still haunts me
but I left that behind with no regrets
Her funeral won't have a single mourner

The memories will always remain
They taint every inch of it well
I wish they'd vanish without a trace

Nearly drove me insane
The core of my own personal hell

My birthplace, Mesa

I will never go back
It holds no power over me
Surviving its worst made me strong

My life now on track
I can clearly see
now I am right where I belong

Satellite Eye

The satellite eye
captures an overview
of a house which looks
foreboding from the outside
But inside, it was a house
of horrors
hoarded to the ceiling now

A childhood and teenage existence
lost and buried under years
of pure pain
My old clothes a moldering pile
by the hot water heater
There's that corner I was beaten in
and a room where I was choked
The walls storing so much sorrow
and anguish that I wish
it would burn to the ground
and release the prisoner
trapped there in time

How did she get away with it?
Abuse, murder, years of lies
but all anyone sees is
a frail, smiling old woman
No one knows how dangerous
this snake is
A rattlesnake, not a boa
Appearance deceptive
You get too close
and realize too late
as fangs puncture your jugular

Release me, witch!
I left you in the dust long ago
the memories I have been forced to carry
Take them!
You can lie in misery
with the memories of
what you did
so they remind you
why you'll always be
afraid and alone
and why you have
no power over me
I am free
and I'll never be anything
more than the 'me' I am

Spiderwebs*

She tried to steal the spotlight
sitting so high above us all
Not caring about wrong or right
as she plotted our family's downfall

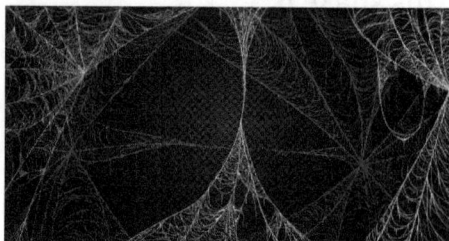

Cagey like a spider
Her presence, unsettling
Nothing was off limits to her
Everyone fair game for her meddling

"Your aunt said this about you"
"Your grandma thinks you're the worst"
It didn't matter whether it was true
she made me believe I was cursed

Spanning out in all directions
Ripples like flows and ebbs
The light caught the invisible reflection
of all her spiderwebs

She knew her only hope
was to keep us all apart
I thought she might change, but nope
She reveled in breaking my heart

Once my aunt and I

were able to see through her lies
I couldn't fathom just why
she never stopped cutting me down to size

I guess doing my father in wasn't enough
sending him six feet below
just to prove she was tough
My mother, the Black Widow

She enjoyed the misery she caused
Thinking no one could see through her charade
Each time she'd spin another web, I paused
Realizing what an impenetrable wall she'd made

After learning the truth, I tried to reach out
I wrote to my dad's mom, who I had never gotten to meet
I was filled with doubt
Would she be mean or sweet?

I got a phone call back from an aunt I'd never met
She told me I'd missed my grandma by 8 months
She had died…and I'd never get
to even hug her once

I did make it out there in time
to meet my Grandpa Herb
Got to drink margaritas with fresh lime
while we sat out on the curb

My aunt told me that Grandma Lola had been looking for me
She had wanted me in her life
but I was the one person she didn't get to see
All because of my father's wicked wife!

One day, justice will be done
She'll be judged by the highest power
God, who sees everyone
who can see every day, minute or hour

Once she's answered for her sins
those plagued by her will have a brand-new day
and we'll all be wearing our biggest grins
as we brush those spiderwebs away

*This poem was first published in Volume 32 Issue 2 of "Fine Lines" magazine in July 2023. Big thanks to David Martin for selecting this poem to include with so many other talented poets' works!

The Revelation

I believed you when you said I was beautiful

and when you told me you would love me forever

I soon felt like the biggest fool

when our connection you did sever

All your lies melted away

in the clear light of honesty

The moment I heard you say

that I needed you more than you needed me

Your words installed doubt in me

I never wanted to trust again

I cried out to God on bended knees

to stop allowing me to fall for dishonest men

Doubting I could ever make it without you

kept me stuck over a decade and a half

But once I saw I could make it through

I couldn't help but laugh!

You're the one who said I needed you more...

but in fact, the truth is hilarious to tell

Your life without me became a burdensome chore
and my rise to freedom was your descent into hell

You stole my house from me
then couldn't qualify to refinance it
I wondered how stupid you could possibly be
while noting everything you touched after the divorce turned to shit

You sold it a year too early
barely made enough to cover buying your new place
60 more pounds that don't make you burly
but that do make you look like a disgrace

Picked a crook for a home builder
They stole your down payment
You lost any filter
and just whined about your torment

You lived for 2 years in a camping trailer
on an obscure plot of land
You stood proudly as your own life's derailer
pretending everything was still going as planned

while you fought to get your down payment back
and find a new contractor
You never kept track
of your wild spending with a calculator

You owed 10 grand to the IRS
Trailer and truck took turns breaking down

By that point, it was anyone's guess
if your face could do anything besides frown

Although I believed you at first
that I might not make it on my own
I began to feel like someone freed from a curse
knowing any seed of mine sewn

would yield wonderous fruit
Graduated from college with a 4.0
Shed 30 pounds from my birthday suit
Got a job with almost double the pay working from home

Found the love of my life
and a bigger house to rent
I became the lucky wife
of that wonderful gent

Checked off some of my bucket list things
Dream vacation and a million pics
Self-publishing my book, which made my heart sing
Knowing because my husband exists, not all men are dicks

So, looking back, who needed who?
Clearly you needed me
but now you're screwed
and I'm free!

You'll keep weaving your tale for pity
which I don't care to hear

I've moved to a new city
where my future is bright and clear

Realm 2: Still Mental

      In the ups and downs of everyday life, one thing that remains constantly present (whether controlled by medication or not) is mental illness. I am not ashamed to say that I have several forms of mental illness, as does my husband. Our love is such a rare and beautiful thing...but when a depressed, anxious, PTSD stricken girl meets a Schizoaffective with Bipolar 1 type guy, you have no choice but to take a deep look inside yourself and figure out what 'okay' really means to you. You keep working at it until you get it. Thankfully, he and I have found our 'okay' together. So, the poems in this realm are a little on what some would say the 'depressed side' of me, realizing that there is hope. Some of them show how I manage some of my symptoms, particularly in the poem, "Fear".

Bipolar Gemini

He broke sobriety

and fell out of bed

and he laid there in his entirety

with a bump on his forehead

Afterwards, his mind was scrambled

Definitely Bipolar Gemini

Listing all his sins, he babbled

leaving me sitting there asking why

He said he never loved me

and our marriage was a mistake

but in his eyes I saw clearly

through the awful pain I had to take

He had been cheating on me

but didn't know why

his love for me, he couldn't see

my Bipolar Gemini

We should get a divorce!

It's a lie!

You can never force

true love to die

His illness does not define him

It's a torture for him, too

but better or worse, I stick by him

despite what he put me through

If I would have thought

he had control of his mind

when he was caught

then it may mean leaving him behind

His mind a mess of confusion

Bipolar Gemini

Icing his contusion

as I lift my tear-streaked face to the sky

I'm not beautiful

I'm not okay

embarrassing and awful

time to be thrown away

But again, his eyes betrayed

and I knew it was a lie

and that he never meant to stray

My Bipolar Gemini

A new day on the horizon

means forgiveness and healing

never again will he have to run

to avoid things with which he's dealing

This all happened so fast

I still wish I knew why

but I do know my love will always last

for my Bipolar Gemini

All this pain

This huge lie

Logic wished for in vain

for my Bipolar Gemini

Now it's behind us and we stand strong

Our feet on the foundation of love

He told me I did nothing wrong

and I thanked the heavens above

I wish for this to never come back

this exhausting, monstrous lie

and for there to never be another crack

in my Bipolar Gemini

Fear*

We're in this together

but you don't see it that way

To you, I am just something uncomfortable

that needs to leave

The more you try to push me out the door

the more I strengthen my grip

and double down

I know I'm exhausted

this useless back and forth

You insisting I go

me insisting I am where I belong

You see, the problem is not me

it is how you see me

To you, I am an enemy

to be conquered

If you would only open your eyes

and see that I am a part of you

You will never be able to

get rid of me

All I need

all you need

is one simple embrace

from one another
Take me in your arms
so that I subside
Tell me that you understand
I am not trying to hurt you
I need reassurance too

how calm I feel now
You understand me
which is so disarming
I will keep my name the same
but it will stand for something more
Next time you think
that you may
Forget Everything And Run
just take a deep breath
and instead we'll work together
to Face Everything And Rise

*This poem was first published in the online publication "Put It To Rest" on Medium in April 2023. A huge hug to Lindsay Soberano Wilson for helping me share this with so many others!

Filed Away

So many memories
filed away in my brain
Volume after volume
Shelf after shelf
A library of my lifetime
all in order
Chronological not alphabetical
Each day a new volume is collected
Many years from now
I will realize that tomes
have been misplaced
some are very hard to find
and some have been lost
Maybe that is the mind's way
of making room for all
the new volumes to come
New spaces that I can
keep new memories
filed away in my brain

Fragments of My Mind*

Taking a look inside

I see the broken pieces trapped within

Secrets I've spent a lifetime trying to hide

Change must start somewhere, but how do I begin?

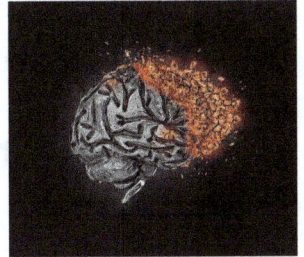

So many fragments of me

Each with a different face

Each one of them can see

that I can't keep up this pace

The inner child wants a childhood

The serious 'me' wants discussion

All of us just want a life that's good

without any repercussions

The angry 'me' wants to release its rage

The balanced 'me' wants more faith

All of us want freedom from this cage

away from the darkness that lurks like a wraith

The wilder 'me' wants a huge dose of fun

The main 'me' at times wishes to be whole

piece together all these fragments

so I can feel like I have a soul

I want to stop being afraid

I want to believe I can change

Time to clean up this mess I made

and prepare to turn the page

This story isn't finished

There's still so much to tell

Once my illness has diminished

and I'm freed from this self-made hell

Piece them all together again

These fragments of my mind

Once that's complete, that is when

I can leave this pain behind

*This poem was first published online in "Put It To Rest" on Medium in April 2023. It was then captured in a YouTube video and recited by internationally renowned and published poet, Michael Lee Johnson. It was then published in Volume 32 Issue 2 of"Fine Lines" Magazine in July 2023, before being published in "Imspired" magazine in Issue 24 in August 2023 and the Volume 12 Print Edition which was released at the end of September 2023.

<u>Mind's Eye</u>

Out of focus
Overexposed
Not in frame

Hocus Pocus!
Perfectly posed
with a new name

Pixelated
Low resolution
Blurry yet illuminated

Overrated
Mind pollution
Obscuring my view

Shutter click
Stunning flash
Brilliant smile

Mine to pick
the rest I'll stash
away for a while

My brain plays tricks
Its camera fails
to capture the real me

It gets its kicks
deflating my sails
Leaving me becalmed at sea

The picture clearly
depicts regret
and sorrow

Yet I love it dearly
because I know I get
a chance of a better shot tomorrow

September*

September is tainted
so devastated, I fainted
Fall to my knees in agony
This isn't how it was meant to be!

I tried so hard not to believe
the words hurled at me that did
cleave
my heart in two, murdering my love
I cried out for help from the heavens above

"Help him!" I begged aloud
"He is trapped in an evil shroud
Save his soul, save his mind
I love him so...I can't leave him behind."

Now that he's been saved
The road to healing has been paved
but the one thing I still can't disguise
is my doubt of what lies behind those eyes

I ask and ask...do you love me?
Just trying to remove evil memories
It's not that I doubt the love is there

as I lay here with my soul laid bare

Please tell me the darkness is gone!

Tell me that I did nothing wrong

I don't want to spend decades getting older

being tortured with shades of bipolar

*This poem was first published in "Put It to Rest" on Medium in May 2023.

Realm 3: Love Conquers All

One observation I have from personal experience is, when you have stood next to someone who is basically fighting hell and their own brain while you stand firm trying to be their light, those with real love for each other come out of those type of situations closer than ever. I know this is true of my husband and me. I think about how lucky we were to have switched therapists and found one who actually knew what the issue was and started helping us to manage it with coping skills (combined with medication). Just me finding him...marrying him...after all of the horrible things which happened to me before him, is the true example of what the phrase 'love conquers all' actually means. Two soulmates who stand as each other's protectors and voice of reason. No stronger bond can be had. Some of these poems were written during difficult times he and I were facing, like his bipolar depressive episode and his alcohol problem (which we finally beat together!) Some of them go on to memorialize our love in words for others to behold. Some touch on the irony of life and how hard we work as parents to make our child's life so much better than ours was, yet fall so short sometimes, despite our best efforts. The important theme of this realm is that no matter what, love always wins!

Daughter

I look at you in wonder
A tiny copy of myself
yet much more mature
than I was at your age
How did you end up
with the same worries
the same fears
which I carry inside me?
The same self-doubt
covering brilliance
Low-self esteem
covering beauty
Anxiety which alienates
your lonely heart
I wanted so much better for you
Your wisdom exceeds
your years
Deep inside your empathetic heart
you worry if anyone
cares as much as you do
Please don't let

your fear of failure
clip your wings
Just know in your heart
that you were meant
to spread your wings
and fly

*Follow Me**

I used to brighten your day,

your face

I used to bring you happiness,

which became my whole reason
for living

Each day I tried to make just a
little bit better,

hoping that I could increase your bliss

and keep shining the light of love

into your heart

But my light no longer illuminates the darkness

I tried so hard to keep at bay

The darkness just absorbs my light -

all that I have to give -

while the blackness grows deeper,

until it starts to turn my light grey

I keep trying to find the light;

someone to shine light into me

to keep this darkness at bay,

but there is no one to do that

It's just you and me

In the dark

Alone

You don't see me,

feel me

anymore

I still see in my mind the wonderful smile

I remember bringing to your face

Right now, memories are my only light

and I am praying their light is strong

enough to guide us out of here!

This is not where we want to be

Nothing can grow or flourish here

Take my hand

Turn around...

...follow me.

*This poem was first published in "Put It to Rest" on Medium in April 2023.

Glass Doors

It's been a lifetime

I've spent with all this darkness

Locked away in a perfect home

The view always inspiring

from behind the glass doors

It made me believe that someday

I would be free

Try as I might, these doors didn't open

so I could come into the light

Every wish I made

to get out of this gilded cage

was like a phone call

straight to your heart

reaching you over the years

My suffering

was like a beacon

drawing you to the desert

When you found me

you saw through the glass doors

which would only open

from the outside

You walked in

and freed me from my cage

The darkness I had been trapped in

passed through the door

like a bad smell

That was the day you found me

and you found your home

within my arms

Hands

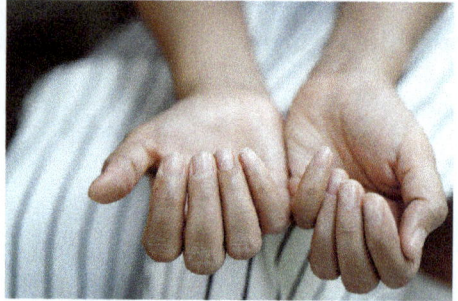

My hands tell my life story

The cracks and dry skin

tell of unceasingly hard work

My nails are bitten down to the nub

which is the result of my anxiety

My knuckle tattoos

show inspiration to all

The caress of my rough hand

against your smooth cheek

when you are sad

is somehow soft in contrast

What my hands truly are

is a safe place

where you entrust your heart

and where I gladly hold love

in the palm of my hand

Hold On

When I was trapped
in monstrous relationships
Enduring horrors
I prayed to God to save me
and his reply was
"I'm moving the pieces
and getting you there
just hold on to me
and you will be fine."

As time went on
I grew impatient
and said to the Lord
"How much am I
supposed to take?!
This is awful
So awful that
I don't want to live
anymore if this is
the way life is
going to be!"

This time, the Lord
looked at me somberly
and said "Just hold on to me

and don't let go.
We are almost there."
My faith waning, I held on
tight and kept praying
to be free from
this tar pit of evil
in which I was mired

I began to lose hope
until one day
the pit was gone
and I was out of it
but filthy
I asked God to help
clean me up
and the Lord said simply
"Hold On."

As my patience grew
I noticed that
I was clean once more
and furthermore
I was also not alone
and was thankful

One day, the Lord brought
someone to me
I did not recognize him
at first, but the longer
I was around him I realized
this was my soulmate
the one I had prayed

so long for
I began to feel unworthy
in his presence because
of all I had endured

I asked the Lord simply
"What do I do now?"
and the Lord smiled
at me and replied
"Hold on to him
and don't let go.
Now you both
have me watching
over you."

I smiled and
grabbed the hand
of my one true love
When he asked where
we were going
I smiled at him and
said, "Just hold on to me.
Wherever we're going
we're going there together."

I held the Lord's hand
in one hand and
my love's in the other
and I sighed knowing
in that moment that
I was the safest
I had ever been

The Lord looked at
us both and said,
"Let's go!"

I Rejoice*

I rejoice

for the transformation

my life has taken

from a dark and desolate

wasteland;   frightening   and
stagnate

to a chrysalis-wrapped fate

I rejoice

for the turn of fortune

that changed my love life

from a hopeless shackled lie

to a thriving and warm hug

where I am loved as a treasure

I rejoice

for although I had

a rough four decades

I am a bloom

which thrives because

of the fertilizer

life mired me in

I rejoice

for the first time

in my life

my family is not a charade
but a true portrait
of what it means
to be loved

I rejoice
knowing I finally found peace
and it did not require my death
to achieve it
but rather was manifested
into reality

I think of how far
things have come
and treasure every moment
in which I live
Every time I wake up
I rejoice

*This poem was first published in "Put It to Rest" on Medium in June 2023.

Look Up*

Trapped like a genie
when the bottle sucked me in
Shackled and needing to escape
It feels good
until it feels bad
I'm relaxed
until I'm jumping out of my skin

You lied to me!
You said the answer was within
but all I found was a trap
Time kept moving around me
If anything changes, it was for the worst
The voices are laughing at me
They think I've lost this fight

I'm ashamed
I wish everyone would leave me alone
I'm scared
I wish someone would hold my hand
I thought I needed you
but all I really needed was me
to find me
to love me
to help me

I'm no longer digging a bottomless pit
while hypnotized in a trance
shovel in hand
I can see where I am now
I can look up and see the way out
to freedom
to a better me
to life; one where I have the control

I have hope
I have plans
I have a life that has been given to me
a second chance
to do all the things
I never thought I could do

All I needed to do was look up
so I could see and reach for
the hand which has been stretched out
all along to pull me to safety
The hand up helps
but only because I reach for it

*This poem was first published in "Put It to Rest" on Medium in April 2023.

Saved

Shivering and huddled
in the corner of a dumpster
frightened and abandoned
He was drawn to
her whimpering
He lifted her out
of the dumpster
thinking to himself
"Who would throw
this kind creature away?"
He took her home
gave her attention
and love – real love
He saved her life
and her blue eyes
sparkled with light
that had never shone before
She knew she would never
end up discarded again
So, she laid her head
on his chest, listening to

his steady heartbeat
and thanking God
that she had a home
at last
She is me
My life began at 40
The day my future husband
found me and promised
to heal my heart...
and he did!

Treasure

Beautiful eyes of earth
Gold beams from your hair
One who brings so much mirth
A treasure, so rare

A smile that could
bring back the dead
You're captivated by me as if you would
devour every word I've said

Your lips are rose petal soft
Your face, beyond compare
I am transported on love, aloft
by a treasure, so rare

You hold me, and I pause
You kiss me, and I melt
Catching my breath, I was
reeling from all I've felt

You hold my face in your hands
You tell me you'll always be there
Our love, immune to time's sands
because it is a treasure, so rare

Twin Souls*

Take my hand, my love!
Feel my heart beat your name
Hold me in your arms, my love!
With you, I never carry shame

If I could unzip you
and crawl inside, burrowing in
I'd still never be close enough to you
Love is a game I thought I'd never win

But look at you, my love
Your smile is the sun
Your eyes are the stars, my love
Our fates joined as one

The gun in your hand will kill me
The pills in my hand will kill you
Oh, my love, can't you see
we're in this together, through and through

There is no suicide
There is no 'I give up'
Not because there's not pain inside
but because our love is too tough

Your love is the breath in my lungs
Your kiss is the fire in my blood
Every breathless moment, every twirl of the tongue

Is picking me up out of the mud

Your love has saved me countless ways
There's no part of you that you hate which isn't connected to me
We live every one of our days
knowing nothing more perfect than our love could ever be

Ever since the day you took my hand
and I in turn took your name
both of us have been able to take a stand
knowing nothing would ever be the same

You'll never be the one they whisper sideways about
judged to be dark without being heard or seen
You'll never have a reason to doubt
a queen's love for her king

I'll never be the one they whisper sideways about
judged to be worthless without a reprieve
I'll never have a reason to doubt
because your pure love could never deceive

Hold my hand, my love!
You are my very life
Never stop believing, my love
I am more than just your wife

Your wisdom gave strength to my bones
Your embrace set my eyes aflame
If I lost you, God and everyone knows
I could never be the same

This life was made for two
A promise from you to me
I know we'll make it through
and I can't wait for you to see

When your mind is clear
and peace has found your heart
You won't want to be anywhere but here
because you'll know we can never part

It would be like ripping out my own heart
Tearing out my own lungs
Losing a race which I could never start
Slicing through my own ladder rungs

You cut a vein, and I bleed
You walk into traffic, and I'm launched in the air
You're all I could ever need
and you may not think it's fair

On the days things are too tough
and you feel you can't take anymore
When things are just too rough
and your tortured mind is looking for the door

Just remember that when I cried each night
after every beating at the hands of the cruel
When I hoped and prayed I might
someday get to stop playing the fool

Those words were heard by God, but said to you
in the hopes that you could feel that I was here
Here to give you the love you needed, too
and make every cloudy thought disappear

I laid on that closet floor
praying I wasn't breathing my last breath
Praying I'd live to find the door
that would lead me away from death

I found it...I found you
If God wanted either of us dead, we'd still be where we were
Remembering all we went through
that pain mixes into a blur

You are me, and I am you
Punch yourself and watch me fall!
If you see what you're putting me through
then know you're made of my love and stand tall!

When I am sad, you cry
When you hurt, I feel it
I lift my tear-stained face to the sky
knowing you're both the cause and the only way to heal it

You are every one of my dreams
while I am every one of your goals
Remember at times when things might not feel like they seem
we are more than a couple, we are Twin Souls

This chapter of our lives is still empty
That's a gift to never throw away
I hope now that you can see
I'm your tomorrow, but you're my today

*This poem was first published in "Put It to Rest" on Medium in April 2023.

Realm 4: Say it Loud!

When you finally realize how valuable you are and always have been, things start to take a turn for the better. You stand up, put your shoulders back, and are proud to shout your declarations! These poems are in the very heart of this expression. Some of the poems reflect back on my days as a prisoner of abuse at the hands of the cruel. It doesn't matter if whoever hears your voice doesn't understand the message or doesn't agree with it. What matters is that you had the guts to say it and that you believe it to be true. It feels wonderful to be able to be at peace with your feelings and viewpoints. Knowing exactly who and what you are...and what you're not. What you will accept, and what you won't. This realm has one focus: Your statement...say it loud, say it proud!

Following Greatness* **

Strolling with Frost
on the road less traveled
Reassuring Poe
his nightmares will
plague him nevermore
I fell into Whitman's
leaves of grass
and picked myself up
to continue the trod
through Longfellow's
footprints on the sands of time
Johnson and I
hear the echoes of
the change of seasons
My only unwanted companion
being the shadows in my mind
reminding me of just
how black the darkness was
which I survived
Each time when I thought
it was the end
when I fell into nothingness
as a way to save myself from

all the pain which I

remained trapped in

Poet voices would whisper to me

"You've got this!

You are one of us!"

and so, I jumped up

dusted myself off

and continued my unpredictable journey

through the unknown

ahead of me

on Frost's road

and thank God every day

that this was the path I chose

leading me ever closer

as I am following greatness

*This poem incorporates snippets of poems from: Robert Frost's "The Road Not Taken"; Edgar Allan Poe's "The Raven"; Walt Whitman's "Leaves of Grass"; Henry Wadsworth Longfellow's "A Psalm of Time" and Michael Lee Johnson's "Sundown, Fall".

**This poem was first published in an online video on YouTube in May 2023.

It was then published in the Lothlorian Poetry Journal in July 2023. Big thanks to Strider Marcus Jones for choosing this poem!

Ink*

Both ankles tattooed
I mentioned getting another
He said my limit was three
but that rule just wasn't me
Once I shed my toxic prison
I met the real me
She had scars that run deep
thanks to the abuse he perpetrated
I decided my outer wonder
needed to match my inner splendor

A rose garden of barbed wire
in remembrance that beauty is pain
A dagger which pierces the soul
like all the times I was stabbed
in the back by people
who were supposed to love me
The hourglass of life
trying to make dreams come true
before the clock strikes twelve
and mortality ends with the
last grain of sand

A heart with wings and a halo
demonstrating my love of heaven
A tribute to my dad
who passed away in 2000

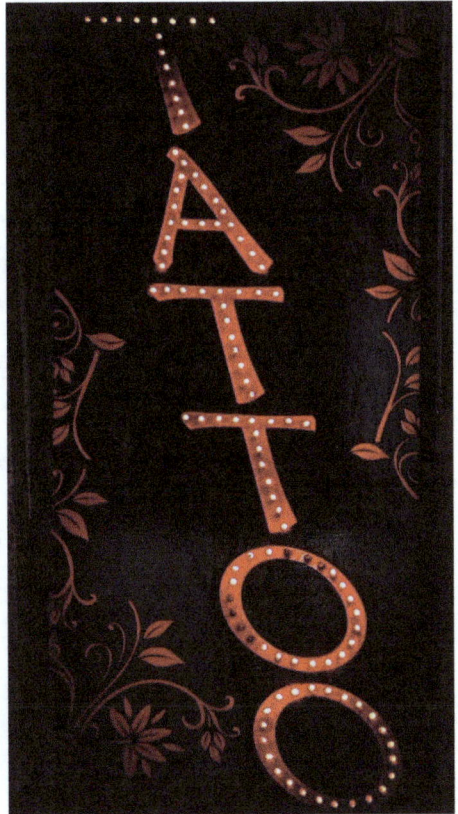

A loud declaration of love
to my soulmate
A dragon, fierce but wise
blowing fire on a pure lotus
Trial by fire, let's go!

My hands carry
the reminder to fear life
rather than death
to guarantee a pleasant afterlife
Gorgeous ankh with a
foreboding ouroboros
representing eternal life
Sleepy Pikachu
dreaming of my children
Alchemist magnesium symbol
representing perseverance

Pentacle formed
from sticks and leaves
giving me connection
to the 5 elements
eternity
and protection from evil
This was inside me all along
The things that make me
who I am
My body a canvas
a walking painting am I
making my statements
showing my scars in plain sight
He didn't destroy me
and he never will

Protection from evil is real

He sees all my tattoos

and his face says

he would never want me back

The ink tells a powerful tale

The ink is magic

because survival runs

in my veins

*This poem was first published in "Put It to Rest" on Medium in June 2023.

Opposition*

Walking in the sunshine
which turns to rain
Picking a flower to smell
which reeks of fertilizer
Running errands
to do something nice
for the one you love
only to have someone
completely minimize
your existence

Sadness grabs for your happiness
Anxiety clutches at your peace
Maddening opposition
when all you want
is the pleasure of
treasuring the simple things
that life has to offer
I refuse to fight a war
which only exists
to exhaust me

My happiness, my peace
It is mine
You cannot ruin it!
You cannot take it!
I say this to the
spiritual and physical
in life

These things cost me
everything to get
and I will not roll over
and let anything take it
This...is my opposition...
to YOU!

*This poem was first published in "Put It to Rest" on Medium in May 2023.

Reflection

I sit and remember
when I couldn't breathe
and life had its grip
around my neck
I take a deep breath
and sigh

Those days are
gone now
In their place
are days of
calm reflection

A mirror to show me
just how far I've come
Dreams of the future
flow through my mind
allowing me to
daydream of more
days of reflection
which are

yet to be

I look at the mirror
and smile
I finally see me there
not a Stepford facsimile
These days, my face
hurts from smiling
rather than from pain
Smile lines gather around
my mouth and eyes

Life for me is reality
no longer a dream
I brush my hair
and sigh
I am right
where I belong

She is Not Me, but I am Her*

Standing here now
The woman before you
is nothing like the 'me' of then

I cannot see how
I survived all I went through
I knew I'd escape, just didn't know
when

I wish somehow, I could go back in time
and talk to my former self
to chisel wisdom into concrete ears

I wouldn't try to change my life
or try to amass wealth
but just try to leave some comfort to pass the years

I still want the life I have now
It's all I could have wished for
and I'm thankful it's mine everyday

But there's a part of me that doesn't like how
behind every closed window and locked door
stood an obstacle in my way

Obstacles make us grow and change
That's not the part I don't see
or why I'd reach out to the me that's malleable

I must ask; I find it so strange
as I look over that past 'me'
Did you know that you're valuable?

Of course, you don't
That is why you gave up
and threw your hopes away

You say you'll try harder, but you won't
All you say is "how high" when someone says "jump!"
You wish for no tomorrow because of the pain felt today

What would I say to her?
That 'me' of 1995 with strong will?
I would gently take her hand

and say, "I know things are horrible, sure
and they'll get even worse, still
but you need to hold fast to your faith

Remember life is a miracle returned to you
This is a blessed second chance
Your decisions will shape the path we walk"

She will know it's true
She will walk away without a second glance
and think, "thanks for the talk"

But the words…they'll take a while to sink in
A seed planted which needs time to grow
into the hedge maze we now traverse

Each time we get lost within
she will come to know
when dealing with time, there is no reverse

The maze is changing behind us
giving us only options forward
Pushing us towards the present

Each time we make a fuss
or try to make the struggles beyond hard
the memory of our talk will be heaven-sent

That wall behind us, made of leaves
pushing against our back
guiding us to the now

cares not for sobs and heaves
cuts no slack
Only knows you must move forward but cares not how

Step after step, year after year
Heartbreak, time and again
Scars that heal, but never stop bleeding

Determination replaces fear
even at times when
she cries she is not getting what she's needing

Do I think she will remember the words?
Will she keep moving on our path
or will she go a different way?

She'll be drawn to what she yearns
But how can you be sure? *Picking leaves off my back...*
...because I'm here, now; with you today

*This poem was first published in the Lothlorien Poetry Journal in July 2023. Big thanks goes out to Strider Marcus Jones for selecting this poem!

The Phoenix*

Take these broken wings!

Let them fall away

Remove the safety net

Let's see how this story ends

I walk the tightrope with eyes shut tight

feeling the danger, but welcoming it

Expecting the moment when

the ground will rush up to meet me

Will that finally end the years of sadness

comparing myself to those I admire

yet always coming up short?

Surely, the answer is no

For, wherever I may go from here

be it good or bad

I will still be me when I get there

with the same fears and insecurities

I'll always wonder why

true happiness eluded me
Why only doubt and apathy
were my constant companions

Why I couldn't see the beauty within me
Why I couldn't allow love to grow as fast as hate did
Why I thought I couldn't handle any of it
Why I decided to give up, knowing it would change nothing

Knowing then that peace can't be achieved this way
I must open my eyes as I walk this fine line
Ignore the ash and soot surrounding me
I must mend these broken wings!

Being reborn does not come only through death
Our choices can breathe new life into us
I must never forget who I am...
...I am the Phoenix, and I will rise again!

*This poem was first published in "Put It to Rest" on Medium in April 2023.

Who am I?

What was I to you?
Just some waiting room before you
found your true destination.
A secretary to book all your
appointments for you

A counselor who listened to all your
petty whining about the life
you lived being miserable,
not seeing that you were the one
who made it that way

A punching bag for you to take out
all your frustrations on
A servant who was supposed to roll over
on demand and do anything
which you asked

Someone who had to stomach your lies,
overlook your faults,

and pretend that I didn't know what
was happening behind my back -
when this fake life you constructed
for us fell apart;

the day you found who you
really wanted and were ready
to discard me like a worthless
piece of trash
Somehow, I was to blame
for it failing.

Despite everything that I did
or was forced to do
by you or for you.
I still caught the blame
Somehow it was my fault
that you never loved me at all
Why did I stick around?
Like I should have known?

Part of me did know, I think
could feel how cold-hearted
you were to my very existence
No sympathy for what I
was going through or
what you put me through.

I was not a person in your eyes...
but an object
which could be possessed
and discarded at will.

That's who I was to you –
a thing with no identity
But who am I?
I am the woman who
was brave enough to
survive you and
all those like you
who tortured me before
you sunk your claws
into me.

I am the beautiful soul
who dreamed of
a better life
so often and so completely
that I manifested it
into being
I am the Phoenix, who couldn't
be destroyed by your
flame of hate
I am and always was
too good,

too pure,
and too loving
to be wasted on
the likes of you

I am the strong survivor
who got up off the floor,
threw that ball and chain
down at your feet,
and walked out the door
without a second glance
I am worth all the love
I get from him, and
all the love never bestowed
on me by the rest

I am worthy
I am alive
I am here to stay,
and there is nothing you
will ever be able to do
to change that

Wounded Knight*

Covering my clay skull
with these threadbare
patches of flesh
Then steadying the
helmet of hindsight
Placing healing salve
on these scorched lungs

Jump starting what
pieces remain of
my heart
so that I can
live life behind
chain mail, metal sheets
and sarcasm

No weapon will
ever penetrate these
barriers again!
Battle scars remain
as does this grizzled veteran
who did nothing more

than try to believe an
open heart would lead
to happiness

No one ever warned
how devastating it can
be when it fails
But alas, this visor
will not raise again
for any man
save the prince
who was promised
to her by
the king who guards
us all

*This poem was first published in "Put It to Rest" on Medium in May 2023.

Realm 5: Just Gotta Laugh!

Laughter is the best medicine, or so they say. Have you ever been able to appreciate humor in everyday life, just in situations or things around you? Most people don't really give it much thought and that is one of the main reasons most of us are stressed out all the time. Life provides us with some really great laugh moments, and none are better than learning to laugh at yourself. If you can laugh at yourself, then some of the sadness or stress of what started out to be a frustrating or unpleasant experience is now something that will leave you with a chuckle! I hope the poems in this realm give you just the laugh you need to feel a little lighter in your heart.

Little Tuxedo

On a walk one day
a small cat walked my way
He was a little tuxedo
and followed me everywhere I'd
go

He had a most urgent meow
which said "I need help now"
He was hungry and very thin
I knew I had to begin

the process of bringing him home
No longer would he have to roam
In the driveway giving him some kibble
He wandered over to take a nibble

He looked up at me as if to say
in a curious sort of way
"What's your name, lady?
I happen to be the real Slim Shady"

So pleased to meet him, I was

and I adopted him because
you don't choose your family
they choose you, and happily

I brought him in to show
him our home and places he could go
He wanted to look behind every door
A curious little guy, to be sure

I love that he's dressed up too
Tuxedo fur through and through
He is very long and lanky
and when he's hungry, very cranky

Bringing him home was the right thing to do
Every time he purrs, it shows he's happy too
Cuteness delivered, he loves to show
off his perfect little tuxedo

Lotion Bar

Christmas in July
all sorts of people
came out for
the event
I sat at my table
working on an autograph
when one of
the vendors came by.
She said (but I did not hear)
that it was a natural
homemade lotion bar
The part I did hear
as she sat it down
in front of me
was that it had
kind of melted a little
I looked down
and saw a small
white owl shaped
item sitting on a piece
of parchment paper
We had been told
there would be
refreshments at
this event
so I thought this was
white chocolate

and I put it in
my mouth
I immediately regretted
this decision and
spit it out
onto the parchment paper
I tasted mint, lemon
and something else
which made it taste
like a bitter chai latte
I winced and looked
up at the vendor
I smirked, humiliated
and pointed to the
parchment paper
"I thought this was
white chocolate and I
tried to eat it."
The vendor said she
had said it was
a lotion bar
but obviously I hadn't heard
that part
"Don't worry," the vendor
said to me.
It is made with
all natural ingredients
so it's not toxic
As relieved as I was
to hear that, I had as
hard of a time
trying to forget
this ever happened
as I did shaking that

strange taste from
my mouth
Lesson learned
Always ask someone
if something they sit
in front of you is
food...just to be safe
and avoid
dreadful aftertastes

On the Floor*

I need a snack

Munchies for TV time

I go in the kitchen

and pull out a skillet

so I can sauté

some chicken

for a salad

I put olive oil

in the skillet

The new bottle

pours out fast

and when I pull back

I spill some on the floor

"I'll clean it up later"

I say to myself

I grab the chicken

from the fridge

When I open the package

juices and meat blood

spurt onto the counter

"Where's a wipe?

I need to clean this!"

I get the bleach wipes

and wipe the counter down

I go to put them away

and accidentally

knock them over

Bleach goes onto the chicken

I pale and realize

now there will

only be salad

I grasp the head of lettuce

and put it on the counter

then get a couple of tomatoes

I wash a tomato

and take it over

to the cutting board

It's slippery and

I lose my grip!

I try to grab

for it

and slip in the oil

on the floor

I go to stabilize

my balance

and end up smashing

the poor tomato

with a squish

I wince; seeds are

between my toes

I reach for the lettuce

so I can chop it up

with the last tomato

and have this

basic salad

My hands, still wet

from washing the tomato

slide on the surface

and launch the lettuce

into the corner of

the kitchen

The corner

which has all manner

of crumbs and dropped things.

I watch it...

you guessed it...

hit the floor

and roll

through the oil

then stop in the

joint of the corner cabinets

I shake my head

and exhale,

knowing that this

simple task

was beyond my ability

to execute

I pick up the lettuce

and see Oreo cookie crumbs

a dried piece of

shredded cheese

and many different

colors of cat fur

I shake my head again

as I look over

the kitchen floor,

which lost the

Battle of the Salad,

as did I

People don't believe that

diets are hard

but the struggle

is real!

I shrug at the mess

"I'll clean this up later.

Guess I'll have to

order pizza.

What a shame!"

*This poem was first published in the Lothlorien Poetry Journal in July 2023. Big thanks goes out to Strider Marcus Jones for selecting this poem!

Pixel

Soft toes
Fluffy paws
Off he goes
to sharpen his claws

Cinnamon swirls
on his orange fur
Back and forth, his tail twirls
He is a cutie, to be sure

Puss In Boots eyes
when it's time for cuddles
When he gets the zoomies, I don't know why
he hunches, runs and huddles

He always knows when you are sad
and is there in an instant to comfort
Sometimes mischievous, but not too bad
He's the loving but rebellious sort

Nightmares sometimes when he sleeps
and bounds away in fear

His tiny meow sounds like little peeps
which is why I hold him dear

This orange cat
is a hyper little angel
and that is why I know that
I'll always love my Pixel!

Pretty Kitty

Small head, tiny eyes
Black fur, confused meow
Suspicious when she spies
Does she know she's a cat now?

Pretty Kitty, my sweet girl
Chunky little Bombay
Try to give catting a whirl
What new things will you try today?

Why does she eat so much?
She's never missed a meal
I reach out to give her belly a touch
while she's flipped on her side like an elephant seal.

Her backside is so massive
Perhaps she ate another cat?
No, she's definitely way too passive
so the truth is…she's pretty fat!

Waddling as she walks
but stepping deliberately, like wearing heels

When in the right mood, she even talks
and we try to guess how she feels.

She rubs against everything
She wants to claim the whole place
While two of the other cats lay waiting
to bite her in the face!

She never gives up hope
that one day, they'll love her too
She's forever my little dope
Pretty Kitty, I love you!

Sketch

She's been his cat
from day one
planted firmly
in my husband's lap
rubbing her face
against the stubble
on his chin

She knows nothing
of personal space
Her fur is wiry
the 1970's multi-brown
carpet remnants
all strung together
in a cat-shaped pattern

She knows how to
say some human words
and does so often
outside my office
or bedroom door

A string of demands
pours from her
furry lips
Scratch, scratch
at the door
She begs for
my husband to
appear immediately

"Now"
"Hello?"
"Michael"
Unmistakable clear words
She has claimed him
as her own
She has tried
many times
to trip me
on the stairs

She plots to
end me
so she can have
him all to herself
Obsessive love
with foul fish breath

She seeks to spread
her mold-like cat fur
on every conceivable surface
This is her house
and I just live in it

Sketch, you're my
oldest cat
with the biggest heart
hidden behind
patchwork fur
and I don't know
what I'd ever do
without your
ridiculous antics
Mold on, dear one
Mold on

The Art of the Fart

Dinner is served

Setting the stage

for the upcoming performance

He savors the meal

and kisses me

with a 'thanks'

As he sits down

to relax for the night

The concert is

about to begin!

It starts off with

a loud growl

The stomach is angry

Then, as the show progresses

A stunning symphony unfolds

Trumpets in C

Trombones in D

various beats of the drum

I glance over in concern

as the audience is overwhelmed

by the performance

Quiet envelops the room

to build anticipation

and before you could

snap a finger

the next cacophony

has been expelled

I'm not sure

whether to hide

or to applaud

these sounds from his bod

Of course, I knew

from the start

there would be

an encore presentation

of his art

The art of the fart

The Scale

Stumbling out of bed
approaching with trepidation
Yesterday's result was
not so bad
What will today bring?
Wincing, I step onto
the treacherous scale
and peer down with
one open eye
The scale spits
its truth
Well…today can't be
a great day now!
I must be vindicated!
This scale projecting these lies!
How blatantly offensive
this device is!
It plays games with
your mind
The hopes it gave yesterday
are dashed today

I'm starting to think
that it has to be
malfunctioning
It's the only explanation
for numbers coming
at me in this combination!
I should throw it
for its betrayal!
Well, enough sulking!
Off to get my
morning donut
and chai latte!

Realm 6: Eternity

So often, our minds will wander into the stars. Galaxies, planets, asteroids…all larger than us and some as old as to have seen the dawn of time. It is those times, when my mind wanders, that some 'spacey' or 'abstract' poems will fill my head and vision with only the kind of wonder that the thought of eternity, the heavens and the creation we live upon can generate. Are we alone out there? Or do we have a creator, watching over us? My poems in this realm answer that question according to my beliefs. There is so much more out there than just stars! Feel free to draw your own conclusions.

Celestial

Celestial creation
Muse of light
I feel all
I see all
Empathetic core
Comfort of ages
Infinite wisdom
Cathartic heart
Constellation arms
Present before time
was time
Doubt has no place here
Love just is
We are one
Strength of eons
Breeze clearing the horizon
Rain cleansing the soul
You are with me
I will never leave you
dear celestial

Elementals

Ignorant flame
Wasted water
Oblivious air
Crumbling earth
Elementals unaware
of how much
they are needed
They may know little
but they know more
than us
Millennia of existence
Basic complexity
Nonchalant presence
If they were not here
since before time
was time
Existence may have
ceased to be
may have never been
Us in the dark
with our breath
naked and afraid

trembling at every sound

which come from

all things and nothing

The moment of creation

Important always

despite the Elementals, unaware

Forever Times Infinity

When I say I
want to spend
forever times infinity
with you...
what does that mean
to you?
Do you realize it
means as long
as existence is,
for as long as
our souls continue
in eternal orbit,
and as long as
time is time
Forever continues on
in perpetuity
Infinity has no end
These two halves
of the same whole
are what help us
to dream about what

and who is waiting
for us in the afterlife
I know that even if
one of us passed
away from this life
that our next evolution
of life is eternal
and cannot be stopped
by anything
other than our creator
who wouldn't stop
it because he has always
wanted us to be
eternal beings
So once we occupy
that energy
inside that space
we know the only
surprises waiting for
us are the ones we
make for ourselves
No more pain or taxes
or broken-down cars
Just us living in our
own definition of perfection
together
Always

Just you and me
That is what
forever times infinity
means to me

*Hourglass**

One tiny grain of sand

For every tear I've shed

Every punch that landed

All the times my heart broke

Each time I was brought to a lower low

The grains continued to fall

Somehow it feels like time slows to a crawl in misery

And pours out faster in the light of joy

I know I'll never stop the sand

There's no chance to flip the hourglass of life

When the sand runs out

And we finally leave this world

Ashes to ashes and dust to dust

My hourglass will shatter

Releasing my spirit

Paroled from my mortal sentence

Ready to begin life everlasting

Free of the constraints of time

Only peace is possible in this place

Outside the hourglass

*This poem was first published in the Lothlorien Poetry Journal in July 2023. Big thanks goes out to Strider Marcus Jones for selecting this poem!

Realm 7: The Little Things

There is no question: the little things in life can occupy our thoughts and bring us a kind of wonder or peace that we otherwise wouldn't have if we did not take the time to take stock in all the seemingly mundane stuff around us that turns out to be something much more. Those little moments, the ones you can capture and hold on to...those are the times to treasure. They might seem routine and able to be observed anytime, but none of us know how much time we have to ignore these little wonders before we have missed them entirely, forever. These poems are dedicated to the little things in life. Simple, yet complex – the things that we don't even take the time to acknowledge that we enjoy or think about.

Arizona, My Home*

Born into the desert heat
The Valley of the Sun
So many people to meet
Winter wonders, summer fun
In Arizona, my home

Saguaros standing tall and proud
telling their decades long tale
The mountains cast their rocky shroud
over every dune and vale
In Arizona, my home

The sunsets take your breath away
As purple fades to royal blue
You sit and reflect on your day
While watching the scattered stars, too
In Arizona, my home

Morning sunrise to start things right
Temperature rising, sometimes a lot
Those born here will understand the plight
of quickly glancing about for a shady spot
In Arizona, my home

I can't believe it's 118!
Seems more like an oven than a locale

But beats all others I've ever seen
We don't have the humidity, like So Cal
In Arizona, my home

All my life, I've only known the desert
The cacti, lizards and Palo Verde trees
Tumbleweeds, rocks and dirt
Ant bites and scraped knees
In Arizona, my home

I'm staying put until the end
I will go out as I came in
Grateful for beauty I can comprehend
and the joy which lies secretly within
Arizona, my home

*This poem was first published in Volume 32 Issue 1 of "Fine Lines" Magazine in March 2023

Cabernet*

Watching the sun-kissed vine
give birth to the grape
Carefully selected and prepped
Squashed into paste
to attain its life's blood
Fermented and bottled
Every year a treasured vintage
The grape's destiny fulfilled
Let's raise our glass
in thankfulness
to the fertile ground
for this superior harvest
which yielded a masterpiece
of unblemished Cabernet Sauvignon
The ghost of the grape
looks on, envious of its new form
knowing it is more popular now
than it was on the vine

*This poem was first published in the June 17, 2023, online issue of The Rye Whiskey Review. Big thanks to David and Scott for accepting this poem and giving it life outside of my computer!

Cinderella's Coach

Pumpkin picked

from a pumpkin patch

for a wonderous pie

The pumpkin had whispered

"Pick me"

Knife held aloft to cut

"Help me"

It glowed

Fairy Godmother appeared

grabbing the pumpkin

"But this is mine!

It spoke to me. Twice!"

Fairy Godmother replied

"When it spoke both times

that was to me

I was meant to pick it

It implored me to save it

from you

This pumpkin

will be given to Cinderella

to change her life

A bit more important

than a wonderous pie"

Morning Ritual

Half asleep, I stumble
towards my teal Keurig
I power it on and
listen to it screech
and whistle like
a tea kettle
Finally, it's ready!
I put my pod in it
and press start
with impatient expectation
I am instantly rewarded
with the caffeinated
Arabica grounds
wafting through the
air, taunting my
nostrils with wakefulness
Mug filled, I reach into
the fridge for the
blue bottle of
Rice Krispies creamer
and pour it in my cup

It's only taken a minute
but now I have the coveted
coffee in my hands
I smell caramel, vanilla
and the sweetness
from the creamer
as I raise the mug
to my lips
The morning ritual -
so basic yet
so vital
This lovely tan
liquid is the
life's blood
of any morning

Sunset

I am watching

the sun setting

over the water

All these years,

I've had the

best view

but now as

my eyes grow

heavy, I realize

I should have

appreciated it more

The gorgeous colors

of indigo and flame

kissing the lake

and illuminating

the ducks, who

are floating aimlessly

as am I

Every memory I have

is touched by

those two colors

My body sits uselessly

like a broken-down car

I am simply out of gas

I am ready now

I look one last time

as the sun sets

over the water

capturing the image

in my mind

a picture burned

into my memory

The tired sun

is ready to rest

So am I

I smile briefly

as I see now

the lake

the ducks

I am floating free

above them

This was my last day

and I can see that

the sun has set

over the water

Never will I forget

the last sunset

my eyes beheld

The day the sun

and I

let go

at the same time

Tonight is

my first night

in the afterlife

The days will

pass differently now

but at least

my view

is now vast

I'm now closer

than I've ever been

I think to myself,

"at least I don't

have to let go

of the routine.

Sunrise, sunset."

The Days of Our Lives

Rainy days
wrapped in their shrouds of grey
crying their mournful tears
Thunderclaps overhead
shaking the frightened ground
Lightning streaks across the sky
casting photo flashes of light
illuminating all the somberness below

Sunny days
lit up with their yellow radiance
as the day begins
The temperature climbs
as people swim and laugh
The ice-cold soda refreshing
as we stand around waiting by the grill
for our juicy burger or plump hot dog

Windy days
start with a playful caress across our faces
then gust hair into our half-opened eyes
Tree limbs bend and sway

and trash blows into our front yard
Dust churns under the force
and moves like a thick wall
The powerful hand pushes us inside and
closes the door behind us

Snowy days
the blankets which will never warm us
lay white and powdery on the ground
Snowflakes fall in a dusting to the earth
powdered sugar mounds waiting for a snowball fight
Warm hot cocoa sipped by a roaring fire
as we cast a glance outside at a snowman
who's none the warmer despite the scarf we gave him

Just as each day has its beauty in simplicity
found in the basic, calm pace it can bestow
The feeling can change in an instant
if you must endure too much at once
Extremes don't tend to serve us well
breeding an aversion to
those very moments we could enjoy
now in ruin due to an extreme taking center stage

The same can also be said of our lives
we can endure that which we encounter unaware
But the path is smoother
the ride much more rewarding

upon the epiphany that moderation

can give us way more

than what excess absconds with

Enjoy each moment and take

not even one for granted...

each one of the days of our lives

The River*

Go with the flow, they say
try to let go
Sometimes the pull
is rushing me forward
Cold rollercoaster hands
throw me this way and that
Fear grips until
the inevitable moment
when I am becalmed
Floating as driftwood
without a care in the world
Please stay forever!
Let me just meander aimlessly
in slow peace
Not meant to be
Not for me
Smashing against the rocks
A rude wake-up call
I feign surprise
but suspected all along
I am tossed once more
never knowing when

peace will return

I can't fight it

We're all in it

A part of it

The river of life

*This poem was first published in the Lothlorien Poetry Journal in July 2023. Big thanks goes out to Strider Marcus Jones for selecting this poem!

The Sparrow

He hops without fear

Searching endlessly

for comfort, warmth, shade, food

Still every day, so happy and free

The sparrow gives his greeting chirp

Coming closer to see the offering

A tasty morsel

I look at him and envy his freedom

Knowing that he can escape danger by flying away

No stressful job

or crippling anxiety

No bills to pay

I looked at his fat little body

Why doesn't fat look that cute on me?

How can I mend my clipped wings

so that I may soar the clouds beside him?

Curious, I caught his eye

He cocked his head, confused by my stare

Continued to devour his treat

Then, french fry gone, he flies away

Goodbye, little sparrow

Dip through the clouds for me

Maybe one day we'll meet again

A different time, a different place

When my wings have regrown

I'm one leap away from carefree

I'll remember you tomorrow and smile

Even though I know I'll never cross your mind

Seeing the world through your eyes is a treasure

Waiting

At the station
waiting for the train
Waiting for hours!
Boredom deafening
Why is there nothing
to read?
Then over the loudspeaker
a mournful voice rose
"Today's train stops are cancelled,"
the voice bellowed
I went to the ticket window
made eye contact with the man
and shrugged in bewilderment
"None of the conductors arrived today,"
the man sputtered with a frown
"This will likely mean we're shutting down.
No one wants to pay for their tickets
as you graciously did today.
No one wants to get the magazines ready
here at the station or
aboard the train.

They sit back on their pillows
drinking their colas
waiting to be pampered."
The man paused to reflect
and then uttered thoughtfully
"Everyone has their part to play
in keeping this place going.
The founders must
continue to help others.
That is their role.
The conductor has to
operate the train.
Routes need to be planned out
with variety
and you passengers,"
he concluded
"must show your patronage
and buy your ticket.
If all of us worked together
there would be more trains
more routes possible
so passengers could choose
the one best for them.
When no one invests
money, time, effort
there is nothing
which can move forward."

I pondered his words and nodded
called two of my friends
who in turn each called two
Within minutes, a crowd was
bustling through the door
of the station
I gathered them together
and we formulated a plan
I went back to the ticket counter
and exclaimed to the man
"We can get the train moving now!"
I pointed at different people
in the crowed and announced
"This is our conductor,
these three will distribute magazines,
these two will pass out refreshments
and we're all paying for our tickets."
The man stood there
mouth agape
and asked,
"Why would all of you
come together to help
this train to leave?"
I smiled and replied
"None of us want to be
stuck here.
These people didn't come

today because they knew

the train was not going anywhere.

The train doesn't want to be

stuck here

in a conquerable limbo

cascade effect

where no one gets to their destination

and it doesn't get to fulfill

its purpose.

You don't want to lose

your position here

because some wanted to sit by

and place their work on others' shoulders.

Laziness gets us nowhere.

Thinking we are more important

than others gets us nowhere.

What changed this day

was the desire,

the will

to move forward."

The man smiled

for the first time

in a long time

Our conductor stepped forward

and bellowed,

"All aboard!" with a beaming smile

"Do you know where we're all headed?"

Still smiling, he said,

"Not exactly.

No one ever really knows

where they're going.

All you can do

is take the journey

and when you know

your time on the train

has passed,

move on and explore

your future."

I grinned and boarded the train

About The Author

Desiree Batiste

Desiree Batiste was born in Mesa, Arizona in 1979. She currently lives in Buckeye, Arizona with her husband, Michael and her daughter Kaylee and their four cats: Sketch, Pixel, Trace and Slim Shady.

After surviving abuse at the hands of her mother in her teenage years, then surviving three separate relationships plagued with domestic violence, Desiree still persevered and graduated summa cum laude with her Bachelors of Science in Technical Management with Criminal Justice specialization in 2020.

Writing stories and poetry has been a life long passion for Desiree. She had her first poem published in a small circulation newspaper for children at age 9 1/2, which only fueled her interest in writing. She has been diagnosed with PTSD and several anxiety disorders as the result of her past experiences. She continues with therapy on these issues, but writing has always been very therapeutic for her and she hopes by sharing her poems and stories, she will help others who are in similar life circumstances.

Desiree has more books in the making as well. She is working on her autobiography and a psychological thriller fiction novel.

Books By This Author

The Shaping Of A Diamond

A 27-year journey of harrowing survival and ultimately finding happiness, told through poems. A real, raw look into the author's life experiences and what it was like to find God, find love, and find herself.

www.ingramcontent.com/pod-product-compliance
Lightning Source LLC
LaVergne TN
LVHW021122080426
835513LV00011B/1194